Great Expectations

Charles **Dickens**

Text adaptation and activities by **Derek Sellen**

Additional activities by **Joanna Burgess**

Illustrated by **Alfredo Belli**

Editors: Claudia Fiocco, Rebecca Raynes
Design and art direction: Nadia Maestri
Computer graphics: Stefania Beccati
Picture research: Laura Lagomarsino

Picture Credits:
Cideb Archive; Mary Evans Picture Library: 34; RANK / Album: 35.

We would be happy to receive your comments and suggestions, and
give you any other information concerning our material.
editorial@blackcat-cideb.com
www.blackcat-cideb.com
www.cideb.it

CISQ CISQCERT
TEXTBOOKS AND
TEACHING MATERIALS
The quality of the publisher's
design, production and sales processes has
been certified to the standard of
UNI EN ISO 9001

ISBN   978-88-530-0808-4   Book
ISBN   978-88-530-0807-7   Book + CD

Printed in Italy by Litoprint, Genoa

Contents

The text is recorded in full.

These symbols indicate the beginning and end of the passages linked to the listening activities.

Charles Dickens (1812-70)

About the Author

I'm Charles Dickens, the famous writer.

Do you know any of my books? Some popular ones are *Oliver Twist*, *David Copperfield*, *A Tale of Two Cities*, *Great Expectations*... and more.

Britain, where I live, is a rich country. Other countries in Africa, India and China are part of the British empire. Victoria is the queen, and she is popular with the people.

But there are a lot of poor people in Britain. Most of the rich ladies and gentlemen don't worry about them, but I feel sorry for the poor people. That's why I write my stories. I want to show that money isn't important, and that poor people can be better than rich people.

In my story, Pip is a good boy when he is poor, but then he changes. At the end of the book, Pip learns that money isn't everything. Read my story – do you agree with me?

BEFORE YOU READ

1 VOCABULARY

A Match the following people (1-3) with the correct definition (A-C).

1 ☐ prisoner
2 ☐ soldier
3 ☐ enemy

A A person who is not a friend.
B A person who is not free because they did something wrong.
C A person who is in the army.

B Label the pictures (1-6) with the correct word from the box.

grave	handcuffs	scar	churchyard	chains	marsh

1 _____

2 _____

3 _____

4 _____

5 _____

6 _____

The Characters

I'm **Pip**. I'm an orphan I haven't got a mother or father.

I'm **Estella**. I'm very beautiful. I haven't got a mother or father, so I live with Miss Havisham.

I'm **Biddy**. I live in the same village as Pip.

I'm **Miss Havisham**. I'm an old lady. I hate men!

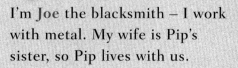

I'm **Joe** the blacksmith – I work with metal. My wife is Pip's sister, so Pip lives with us.

I'm **Bentley Drummle**.
I'm rich and handsome. [1]

I'm **Mr Jaggers**. I'm a lawyer
– I work for rich people.

I'm **Wemmick**.
I help Mr Jaggers.

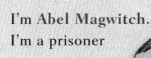

I'm **Abel Magwitch**.
I'm a prisoner

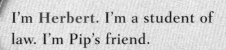

I'm **Herbert**. I'm a student of
law. I'm Pip's friend.

1. **handsome** : attractive, good-looking
(generally used for men).

CHAPTER ONE

The Prisoner on the Marshes

Pip was a young boy who didn't have a mother or father. He lived on the marshes, near the great River Thames. One day he was sitting in the churchyard. He was looking at his parents' graves. Suddenly someone came close to him. It was a prisoner. He was escaping from the prison ships on the river. Pip was very afraid.

Prisoner: I want food. Get me some.

Pip: Y-y-yes, sir. Are you very hungry, sir?

Prisoner: Yes, I am. And bring me a file.[1] I want to cut these chains. But don't tell anyone!

Pip: No, sir!

---

1. **file :**

The Prisoner on the Marshes

Pip ran back to the house. He lived with his sister and her husband, Joe. They were poor people. Joe was the village blacksmith and he was very kind. He loved Pip. But Pip's sister was not kind, and she was often angry. She liked hitting her little brother.

In the middle of the night, Pip stole [1] some food from the kitchen for the prisoner.

You're a bad boy!

Get me some food!

I'm afraid of my sister. But I'm very afraid of the prisoner. It's very bad to steal food. But I must do it. Where is Joe's file? I must take it to the prisoner.

1. **stole** : past simple of *to steal*.

Pip got up early and ran across the marshes. It was very cold and grey but the sun was coming up. He saw another prisoner, who ran away. Pip took the food and the file to the prisoner in the churchyard.

Here's the food. I hope you are not too cold and hungry, sir.

Thank you, boy. This food is good.

Pip: There's another prisoner on the marshes, sir. He's got a scar on his face.

Prisoner: What! He's my enemy! Give me the file. Quick! I must find him.

The Prisoner on the Marshes

Pip went back to the house. When his sister couldn't find the food for dinner, she was very angry. But then some soldiers arrived. Joe had to help them. He had to repair some handcuffs. The soldiers were looking for the prisoners. Joe took Pip to the marshes to watch.

The soldiers found the prisoners. They were fighting because they were enemies. The soldiers took the prisoners back to the prison ship.

First Prisoner: You're my enemy. I want to kill you.
Second Prisoner: You're stupid. Now we're both going back to prison.

UNDERSTANDING THE TEXT

1 COMPREHENSION CHECK

Are these sentences 'Right' (A) or 'Wrong' (B)? If there is not enough information to answer 'Right' (A) or 'Wrong' (B), choose 'Doesn't say' (C). There is an example at the beginning (0).

0 Pip didn't have any parents.
 A Right B Wrong C Doesn't say

1 Pip lived on the marshes, near the castle.
 A Right B Wrong C Doesn't say

2 The prisoner wasn't hungry.
 A Right B Wrong C Doesn't say

3 Joe was married to Pip's sister.
 A Right B Wrong C Doesn't say

4 In the morning, Pip stole some food.
 A Right B Wrong C Doesn't say

5 Pip helped the prisoner.
 A Right B Wrong C Doesn't say

6 The second prisoner was old with grey hair.
 A Right B Wrong C Doesn't say

7 The soldiers wanted to kill the prisoners.
 A Right B Wrong C Doesn't say

8 Joe felt sorry for the soldiers.
 A Right B Wrong C Doesn't say

2 COMPREHENSION CHECK

Complete this summary of Chapter One. Write **ONE** word for each space. There is an example at the beginning (0).

Pip was (0) ....a........ young boy. He lived on the marshes
(1) .... his sister and (2) .... husband, Joe. One day, he
met (3) .... prisoner (4) .... the churchyard. Pip
(5) .... very afraid. He went home and took some food
(6) .... a file for (7) .... prisoner. Pip saw a second
prisoner. This man had a scar on (8) .... face. The two prisoners
(9) .... enemies. They wanted (10) .... fight.

3 VOCABULARY – JOBS
Look at the jobs in the box. They are all from *Great Expectations*.
Label the pictures with the correct job.

| teacher | blacksmith | lawyer | doctor |

1 ☐   2 ☐   3 ☐   4 ☐

T: GRADE 3

4 SPEAKING: JOBS
Joe is a blacksmith. Soon you will meet Mr Jaggers, who is a lawyer.
Talk about jobs. Use these questions to help you.

1   What type of job do you want to do in the future?
2   What do your parents do?
3   What jobs do other people in your family do?
4   Are there any jobs that you don't want to do? Why?

5 E-MAIL
Read this e-mail. Then fill in the information about the film.

○ ○ ○   DON

> Tuesday, 15th August
>
> Sue,
> There is a film of *Great Expectations* at the ABC Cinema in Oxford. It is on today. We can see it at 6.15 or 9.15. Bring £5.00 with you. Then you can buy a ticket and also some popcorn for 50 pence. Meet me at the front door of the ABC. See you there, fifteen minutes before the first film starts,
> Don

0   Name of film: *Great Expectations*   4   City: ....
1   Date: 5   Cost of ticket: ....
2   Times of film: 6   Meeting time: ....
3   Name of cinema: 7   Meeting place: ....

BEFORE YOU READ

1 **LISTENING**

Listen to the first part of Chapter Two. For questions 1-5, tick (✓) A, B or C. There is an example at the beginning (0).

0 Pip went with

A ☐ Miss Havisham.
B ☐ Joe.
C ✓ his uncle.

1 Pip went to

A ☐ Statis House.
B ☐ Satis House.
C ☐ Cat's House.

2 The girl was

A ☐ mad.
B ☐ proud.
C ☐ loud.

3 Estella didn't like Pip's dirty

A ☐ hands.
B ☐ face.
C ☐ boots.

4 Miss Havisham's dress was

A ☐ old and yellow.
B ☐ white.
C ☐ old and black.

5 Estella said that Pip was

A ☐ a gentleman.
B ☐ a blacksmith's boy.
C ☐ beautiful.

2 **READING PICTURES**

A 'gentleman' is a man who comes from a rich and important family. The women from these families are called 'ladies'.
Look at the pictures on pages 15-18 and answer these questions.

1 Can you find any ladies in the pictures?
2 How do you know?
3 Look at the two boys on page 18. How are their clothes different?
4 Which boy is more like a gentleman?

CHAPTER **TWO**

Miss Havisham

A strange, old lady lived in a big house in the village. Her name  was Miss Havisham. One day, she asked to see Pip. So Pip's uncle had to take Pip to her house.

His sister said, 'Miss Havisham is very rich; she's got a lot of money and jewels. [1] You must be good when you're with her, Pip. Perhaps she wants to give you a lot of money.'

Pip's uncle, Mr Pumblechook, took Pip to her house.

It was called Satis House. A young girl opened the gate. She was beautiful, but she was very proud. [2]

Estella: No, I haven't got a mother or father. I live with Miss Havisham and she gives me everything. But don't ask questions, boy!

1. **jewels :**
2. **proud :** (here) someone who is proud thinks they are better than other people.
3. **rough :** (here) in bad condition because of work.

Miss Havisham was sitting in a dark room. She was wearing a very old wedding dress. [1] But it wasn't white — it was yellow because it was so old. There were a lot of clocks, but they didn't work. They all said the same time: twenty to nine.

Miss Havisham: And Pip, do you like Estella?

Pip: She's very beautiful.

Miss Havisham: Pip thinks you're beautiful, Estella.
  So, break his heart! [2]

1. **wedding dress** : when a man and a woman get married there is a wedding. The woman wears a wedding dress.
2. **break his heart!** : when he loves you, hurt him!

Pip often visited Miss Havisham and Estella. Sometimes they played cards and sometimes they sang. But Estella was always proud. Pip began to love her, but she didn't love him. One day Miss Havisham took him into a special room. There was a long table with a very old wedding cake on it. There were spiders [1] and mice [2] everywhere.

> But where is her husband?

> Today is my birthday, Pip. Push me around the table. This is my wedding cake from a long time ago.

Miss Havisham: I hate men. I'm teaching Estella to hate men too, Pip. You're only a boy now. But when you're a man, you must leave Satis House for ever.

Pip: But I want to marry Estella.

Estella: Silly boy! I hate you!

1. **spiders :**   2. **mice :**

One day, Pip met another boy in the garden. They fought. [1] The boy fought like a gentleman, but Pip won because he fought like a blacksmith. Estella watched them fighting.

> You're the winner.

> Well done, Pip. You can kiss me if you want.

Pip kissed Estella on the cheek. [2] Later, Miss Havisham said goodbye to him.

Miss Havisham: This is the last time, Pip. I don't want to see you here again. Here's some money. You must be a blacksmith.

Pip: But I want to see Estella again. I love her!

Miss Havisham: I'm sending Estella to Paris. She'll become a lady. But you're a blacksmith, Pip. You must work with Joe Gargery.

---

1. **fought** : past simple of *to fight*. 2. **cheek** : the side of your face.

UNDERSTANDING THE TEXT

KET

1 COMPREHENSION CHECK

Read this summary of Chapter Two. Choose the best word (A, B or C) for each space. There is an example at the beginning (0).

Pip's uncle, Mr Pumblechook, (0) ...*took*........ him to Satis House. There, he met a young girl and (1) .... old lady, Miss Havisham. Miss Havisham (2) .... wearing an old wedding dress. Some people thought that (3) .... was mad.

Estella was very beautiful, but proud and not polite. Pip wanted to marry her, (4) .... he could not because he was not a gentleman. Pip often visited Miss Havisham. One day, it was (5) .... birthday. Pip saw a long table with an old wedding cake (6) .... it. There were mice (7) .... spiders too. Later, Pip met Herbert and fought (8) .... him.

0	A take	(B) took	C brought
1	A any	B an	C a
2	A was	B were	C is
3	A she	B her	C he
4	A so	B and	C but
5	A her	B hers	C she
6	A above	B on	C in
7	A and	B no	C but
8	A of	B from	C with

2 TELLING THE TIME

All the clocks in Miss Havisham's house said the same time: twenty to nine. Write the times in numbers and words below each clock.

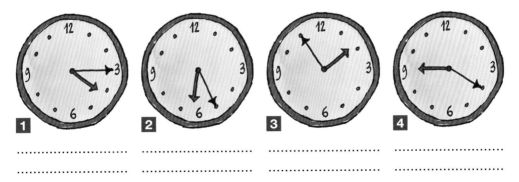

1	2	3	4
....	....	....	....
....	....	....	....

'I MUST TAKE IT TO THE PRISONER.'

We use **must** when it is necessary to do something. The past tense of **must** is **had to**.

3 MUST

A Underline sentences with *must* in Chapter One and Chapter Two of the story.

B Complete the sentences in the list of what everyone must do. Use one word from box 1, one from box 2 and a phrase from box 3 to make sentences with *must*. There is an example at the beginning (0).

1　　　　Estella　Pip (x3)　The prisoner

2　be　clean　fight　~~repair~~　open　take　wear

3　　the ha~~nd~~cuffs　some food for the prisoner
　　Herbert　Pip to Satis House　red uniforms
　　　　　　the prison ship

To do list

0　Joe ...*must repair the handcuffs* ....

1　The soldiers ....

2　.. the gate.

3　.................... go back to ....

4　Uncle Pumblechook ....

5　.................... steal ....

6　.. good at Satis House.

7　Pip ....

8　... his boots.

BEFORE YOU READ

1 LISTENING

Listen to the first part of Chapter Three and answer the following questions.

1　Who are the two people having this conversation?
2　Which three adjectives are used to describe Biddy?
3　What does Pip want to do?

CHAPTER **THREE**

The Money

Pip worked with Joe. He loved Joe and Joe loved him, but Pip was unhappy because he wasn't a gentleman. He was eighteen years old now. When Pip's sister was ill, a young woman came to help Joe. Her name was Biddy. She was kind and she was very pretty. She liked Pip very much, but Pip couldn't forget Estella.

I want to be a gentleman, Biddy. I want to marry Estella. I want to live in London.

I'm happy here with you and Joe, Pip. Joe isn't a gentleman, but he's a very good man.

Pip: Yes, you're right. But...

Biddy: And the marshes are beautiful. I'm not a lady and I'm not rich, but I like my life.

One day, a man came to see Pip. His name was Mr Jaggers. He was a lawyer from London.

Jaggers: I've got some good news for you. You're rich. You've got great expectations. [1]

Pip: What! I don't understand…

Jaggers: Someone wants to give you a lot of money. You must go to London, and you must learn to be a gentleman.

1. **great expectations** : a good future with a lot of money and a good life.

It was a big surprise for Pip. Joe and Biddy were very sad. They didn't want to lose Pip.

Who is my benefactor,[1] sir?

I can't tell you the name.

Pip: Is it a man or a woman?

Jaggers: I can't tell you. Don't ask any more questions. Take this money and buy some gentleman's clothes.

Pip: (*thinks*) Miss Havisham is my benefactor. She wants me to be a gentleman. She wants Estella to be a lady. She wants us to get married! I'm very happy!

1. **benefactor** : a person who gives money or help to another person.

Pip left the village. Joe and Biddy were crying, but Pip was happy. In the coach he was thinking about the future.

Pip: I'm going to London. I can't believe it! I want to see St Paul's Cathedral and Westminster Abbey and the Queen's palace. I've got money. I've got new clothes. I'm a gentleman!

UNDERSTANDING THE TEXT

1 **COMPREHENSION CHECK**
Are these sentences true (T) or false (F)? Correct the false sentences.
There is an example at the beginning (0).

		T	F
0	Pip and Joe worked together.	✓	☐
1	Joe loved Pip, but Pip didn't love him.	☐	☐
2	Pip's sister was called Biddy.	☐	☐
3	Mr Jaggers lived in the village.	☐	☐
4	'Great expectations' meant that Pip had a good future.	☐	☐
5	Pip had to learn to wear expensive clothes.	☐	☐
6	Pip didn't know the name of his benefactor.	☐	☐
7	Pip was sad when he said goodbye to Joe and Biddy.	☐	☐
8	Pip wanted to go to London.	☐	☐

2 **OPPOSITES**

A Match these adjectives from Chapter Three on the left with their
opposites on the right.

1	☐ kind	A	bad
2	☐ ill	B	poor
3	☐ pretty	C	unkind
4	☐ happy	D	happy
5	☐ rich	E	old
6	☐ good	F	well
7	☐ sad	G	unhappy
8	☐ new	H	ugly

B Now complete these sentences using some of the adjectives above.

1 Do you like my .... shoes? I bought them yesterday.

2 He has got a lot of money. He is very ....

3 I am really .... because next week the school holidays
   will start!

4 Helen hasn't got much money and her car is ....

5 My best friend gave me this beautiful present for my birthday.
   She is very ....

6 I ate too much chocolate and now I feel ....

3 WORD GAME

Can you remember the adjectives from exercise 2 A on page 25? Find eight in the word square.

```
U  N  K  I  N  D  F  H  R
L  T  I  P  I  M  C  J  O
G  X  F  N  R  I  Y  T  G
T  D  C  J  R  E  O  M  Q
H  A  P  P  Y  L  T  T  Y
J  L  B  K  S  N  Y  T  Y
O  D  S  I  L  L  B  L  Y
L  Q  T  A  F  G  G  T  K
D  G  R  X  D  U  W  X  X
```

'...BUY SOME GENTLEMAN'S CLOTHES.'

We use the imperative to tell people what to do. We form the imperative from the infinitive of the verb without *to*.

Open the gate.   Don't look at me.

4 THE IMPERATIVE

A   Underline five examples of the imperative in Chapter Three.

B   Put the words (A-I) in the correct order to make imperative sentences. Then write them in the correct spaces in the sentences (1-8). Add *don't* if necessary. There is an example at the beginning (0).

A   me kiss
B   us forget
C   anyone about tell me
D   in come
E   ask name your benefactor of the

F   his heart break
G   handcuffs these repair
H   with fight me
I   good be

0   Estella to Mr Pumblechook: ..Don't come in ....
1   Miss Havisham to Estella: ....
2   Estella to Pip: ....
3   Mr Jaggers to Pip: ....
4   His sister to Pip: ....
5   Soldiers to Joe: ....
6   Prisoner to Pip: ....
7   Herbert to Pip: ....
8   Biddy and Joe to Pip: ....

5 CONVERSATION

Complete the conversation. What does Mr Jaggers say to Pip? Write the correct letter next to the number. There is an example at the beginning (0).

Mr Jaggers: Come to my office in London.
Pip: 0 ..H..
Mr Jaggers: There is a coach every day from Rochester.
Pip: 1 .....
Mr Jaggers: It costs six pence and it leaves at 11 a.m.
Pip: 2 .....
Mr Jaggers: 5 hours.
Pip: 3 .....
Mr Jaggers: Yes. Then you must come to my office.
Pip: 4 .....
Mr Jaggers: Near Newgate Prison, in the centre of London.
Pip: 5 .....

A	How long is the journey?	E	6 o'clock.
B	When does it go?	F	So I'll be in London at 4 p.m.
C	Where is it?	G	Who is it?
D	Thank you. I'll see you tomorrow.	H	How can I travel to London?

BEFORE YOU READ

1 LISTENING

 Listen to the first part of Chapter Four and fill in the gaps with the words you hear.

Pip arrived in London. He saw a **(1)** .... city for the first time. He forgot Joe and Biddy. He only thought about Estella. He went to live in a house **(2)** .... the centre of London, near Mr Jaggers. In the same house, he met Herbert Pocket.
Herbert: Hello. My name's Herbert.
Pip: Hello. I'm Pip. I **(3)** .... you! You're the boy from Miss Havisham's garden!
Herbert: Yes, now I remember you too. But we can **(4)** .... friends now. I want **(5)** .... show you London. My father is a teacher. He can help you to be a gentleman.
Pip: Then I **(6)** .... marry Estella.

CHAPTER **FOUR**

London

Pip arrived in London. He saw a big city for the first time. He forgot Joe and Biddy. He only thought about Estella. He went to live in a house in the centre of London, near Mr Jaggers. In the same house he met Herbert Pocket.

Herbert: Yes, now I remember you too! But we can be friends now. I want to show you London. My father is a teacher. He can help you to be a gentleman.

Pip: Then I can marry Estella.

Herbert: Be careful, Pip. Miss Havisham hates men. Many years ago, she was in love. But, on the day of the wedding, the man didn't come to the church. The time was twenty to nine! Estella hates men too.

1. **curtains :**

Pip learnt to be a gentleman. He learnt to speak like a gentleman. He learnt to eat like a gentleman. Joe visited him in London, but he didn't stay long. Pip didn't want to talk to his old friend, the blacksmith. Pip was a snob [1] now.

Joe: Biddy says hello to you, and hopes you are well.
Pip: Thank you, Joe.
Joe: I'm going back to the village now, Pip. London isn't the right place for me.
Pip: Goodbye, Joe.

1. **snob** : someone who doesn't like people who are not gentlemen.

Joe was unhappy. He loved Pip.

Pip bought new clothes and new furniture. Mr Jaggers always gave him money.

I've got some money for you, Pip. How much do you want?

A lot, Mr Jaggers.

Jaggers: All right, Pip. You're twenty-one years old this year. Your benefactor wants to give you some more money.

Pip: But who is my benefactor? It's Miss Havisham, isn't it?

Jaggers: I can't tell you.

Wemmick: Here's your money, sir.

Pip was very happy. He was a rich gentleman. He could marry Estella!

UNDERSTANDING THE TEXT

KET

1 COMPREHENSION CHECK

Are these sentences 'Right' (A) or 'Wrong' (B)? If there is not enough information to answer 'Right' (A) or 'Wrong' (B), choose 'Doesn't say' (C). There is an example at the beginning (0).

0 Pip was in Rochester.
  A Right   (B) Wrong   C Doesn't say

1 Pip knew Herbert.
  A Right   B Wrong   C Doesn't say

2 Herbert's father could fight.
  A Right   B Wrong   C Doesn't say

3 Miss Havisham got married many years ago.
  A Right   B Wrong   C Doesn't say

4 All her clocks said 8.40.
  A Right   B Wrong   C Doesn't say

5 Joe was happy in London.
  A Right   B Wrong   C Doesn't say

6 Joe didn't know London.
  A Right   B Wrong   C Doesn't say

7 Pip got more money because he was eighteen.
  A Right   B Wrong   C Doesn't say

8 Mr Jaggers didn't tell Pip who his benefactor was.
  A Right   B Wrong   C Doesn't say

2 WHO SAYS IT?

Match a character (A-F) to the sentence they say (1-6).

A Herbert   C Pip   E Mr Jaggers
B Miss Havisham   D Joe   F Mr Wemmick

1 ☐ 'You're a fine gentleman now.'   **4** ☐ 'Here's your money, sir.'
2 ☐ 'But who is my benefactor?'   **5** ☐ 'Stop the clocks.'
3 ☐ 'I want to show you London.'   **6** ☐ 'I can't tell you.'

'MISS HAVISHAM HATES MEN.'

We use the present simple to talk about permanent situations or things that happen regularly.

I always **have** *lunch at 1 o'clock.*   *We* **don't go** *to school on Sunday.*

3 PRESENT SIMPLE

A Read Pip's description of a typical day in his life. Use the verbs in the box to complete the description. The verbs are in the infinitive, you may need to change them. There is an example at the beginning (0).

| need | dance | visit | be | want | ~~get~~ up |
| | tell | be | like | have | live |

I usually **(0)** ...get up. at nine o'clock and I have breakfast with Herbert. We **(1)** .... in the centre of London and in the morning I often **(2)** .... famous buildings like St Paul's Cathedral and Westminster Abbey. Sometimes Herbert comes with me – he **(3)** .... me about the history of London. There **(4)** .... a lot more people here than in my village, it's very different. Joe **(5)** .... London but I love it! After lunch, I always **(6)** .... lessons with Herbert's father. He is teaching me to be a gentleman. Herbert **(7)** .... lessons – he's already a gentleman!
In the evening, we often go to parties with other students. My friends **(8)** .... with a lot of beautiful girls but I **(9)** .... interested in these girls. I **(10)** .... to marry Estella.

We make questions in the present simple using the verb **to do**. This is an auxiliary verb.
Do you **like** this book?   Where **does** Pip **live**?

B Put the words into the correct order to make questions. They are all about Pip's typical day. There is an example at the beginning (0).

0   you live do Where
..Where do you live.. ?

1   Herbert Does with visit you London
.... ?

2   Joe Does London like
.... ?

3   do lunch do What you after
.... ?

4   Herbert Do have lessons you with
.... ?

5   parties do What your do at friends the
.... ?

C Work with a partner. One of you is Pip and the other is the interviewer. Ask and answer the questions in B.

Ladies and Gentlemen

In the eighteenth century, everyone in Britain had a place in society. [1] It was almost impossible to change. If a man was from a rich, important family, he was a gentleman. If a man was from a poor family, he could never become a gentleman. It was the same for women.

But in the time of Queen Victoria (1837-1901) society was different.

Fashionable ladies' evening dresses, from the Englishwoman's Domestic Magazine, January 1862.

Even a poor person, by working hard and becoming rich, could become a gentleman or a lady. It was not easy but it was possible. It was the first time in British history that people could change their place in society.

Dickens himself is a good example. His family was not rich. His father even went to prison because he couldn't pay people who he bought things from. So, only two days after his twelfth birthday, Dickens had to go to work in a factory to help his family.

1. **society** : the people who live in a country, and their way of life.

Alec Guinness as Herbert Pocket and John Mills as Pip in David Lean's film of *Great Expectations* (1946). Pip is wearing exaggerated gentleman's clothes, but he still doesn't eat like a gentleman!

But Dickens began to write and he became popular. He made a lot of money and he became a 'gentleman', and from the 1840s until his death he lived in big, expensive houses.

In *Great Expectations* there is a 'gentleman': his name is Drummle, and you will meet him in Chapter Five. He's from a rich family, but... is he a good person? You will find the answer as you read the book. As a boy, Pip was not a 'gentleman'. Then he went to London to learn how to be a gentleman, but he became a snob. Joe isn't a 'gentleman'. He's poor and he has to work hard, and he can't read or write. But he's very kind and good.

Great Expectations asks the question: which of these men is a real 'gentleman', and why? It also asks us who is a real 'lady': Miss Havisham, who is from a rich family; Estella, who learns to be a lady in Paris; Biddy, who is poor, hard-working and kind?

1 COMPREHENSION CHECK
Answer the following questions.

1 In the 18th century, was it possible to change your place in society?
2 What happened in the 19th century?
3 Did Dickens change his place in society?

PROJECT ON THE WEB

Children in Victorian Britain

Connect to the internet and go to www.blackcat-cideb.com or www.cideb.it. Insert the title or part of the title of the book into our search engine. Open the page for *Great Expectations*. Click on the Internet project link.

In the dossier you learnt about the adults in Victorian Britain. But what about the children?

Divide the class into three groups. Each group can look at a different area: work, play or school. Tell the other groups what you found out. Use these questions to help you.

1 How was life different for children in the 1800s compared to your life?
2 What were the differences between rich children and poor children?
3 Would you like to be a child in Victorian Britain? Why/why not?

CHAPTER FIVE

Estella in London

Estella came back from Paris. She was a lady and Pip was a gentleman. Pip went to visit Miss Havisham at Satis House and met Estella. Pip thought that Miss Havisham was his benefactor.

Miss Havisham: Good. Look, here is Estella.

Pip: You're very beautiful, Estella.

Estella: Ah, it's the blacksmith's boy. You're a gentleman now! Your shoes are clean!

Miss Havisham was happy. On the day of her wedding, a man broke Miss Havisham's heart, so she taught Estella to break the hearts of other men.

Miss Havisham: Is Estella beautiful, Pip?

Pip: Yes, she is.

Miss Havisham: Love her, Pip. Love her, love her, love her!

Estella came to London. She and Pip were friends, but she met and danced with a lot of different men. Pip was jealous. [1] One evening, at a party, he was angry.

> Estella, please don't dance with other men! Don't smile at them. Marry me! I'm a gentleman now, and I love you!

> Don't be silly, Pip. I haven't got a heart. I can't love you. You'll only be unhappy with me.

Gentleman: Do you want to dance, Miss Estella?
Estella: Yes, thank you, sir. Goodbye, Pip.

1. **jealous** : angry and unhappy because somebody you love is interested in another person.

Pip was very sad. Herbert wanted to help his friend, and he told him to forget Estella.

'But I love her,' said Pip. Pip was sitting and drinking with Herbert and some other students. Bentley Drummle was there. He was rich and handsome, but many people thought he was a bad man. He picked up his glass.

Pip was angry. 'You can't drink to Estella. You don't know her.'

To Estella, the most beautiful woman in London!

'Why not? I know her well. She's my special friend. I often dance with her.'

'You're lying.' [1]

Herbert told Pip to be careful. Everyone was listening.

Later, Bentley Drummle got a letter from Estella. He showed it to everybody. Estella wrote,

'Yes, I know Mr Drummle. Sometimes I dance with him. Estella.'

Pip had to say sorry. 'I'm sorry,' he said. 'You're right. You aren't a liar.' [2]

'And you, sir, are not a gentleman.'

The other students laughed at Pip.

Pip went to see Estella.

'Estella, why do you see Bentley Drummle?'

Estella answered, 'I know a lot of men, Pip. I'm very beautiful. Miss Havisham gives me a lot of money. They all want to marry me.'

'But, Estella, Drummle is a terrible person. He's cruel [3] and stupid.'

'I like cruel, stupid, rich men. Remember, Pip, I haven't got a heart.'

---

1. **lying** : not telling the real facts (from *to lie*).
2. **a liar** : a person who lies.
3. **cruel** : wanting to hurt other people.

Biddy wrote a letter to Pip. She told him that Pip's sister, Joe's wife, was dead. Pip went back to the village. After the funeral [1] he spoke to Biddy.

> Joe is very sad, Pip. You never write to him or visit us.

> I'm sorry Biddy. But don't worry. I want to visit Joe often now. My sister is dead and he's alone.

Biddy: But... I can't believe you, Pip. You're a gentleman now and you don't want to remember Joe and me.

Pip: No, Biddy. I remember you all.

But Pip didn't visit them. He only thought about Estella and Miss Havisham. He forgot his real friends.

1. **funeral** : the ceremony for a dead person.

UNDERSTANDING THE TEXT

KET

1 **COMPREHENSION CHECK**

Read this summary of Chapter Five. Choose the best word (A, B or C) for each space. There is an example at the beginning (0).

Estella came back to Satis House and Pip met (0) ...her........... there.
Estella remembered Pip's dirty (1) .... but now he was a
gentleman and he wanted (2) .... marry her. Miss Havisham was
very happy and she told Pip to (3) .... Estella.
Estella went to London but she met and danced with a lot (4) ....
different men. Pip was jealous but Estella told (5) .... that she
didn't have (6) .... heart.
Bentley Drummle, a rich, stupid man, drank to Estella. Pip (7) ....
very angry and called Drummle a liar but later he had to (8) ....
sorry to Drummle. Pip went back to the village for (9) .... sister's
funeral. He told Biddy that he wanted to visit Joe more often but Biddy
(10) .... believe him.
She was right!

0	Ⓐ her	B	him	C	them
1	A hands	B	boots	C	feet
2	A for	B	to	C	at
3	A like	B	live	C	love
4	A to	B	of	C	for
5	A him	B	her	C	his
6	A any	B	a	C	an
7	A was	B	were	C	wasn't
8	A tell	B	speak	C	say
9	A his	B	her	C	hers
10	A did	B	does	C	didn't

T: GRADE 2

2 **SPEAKING: FRIENDS**

Herbert is Pip's friend. Tell the class about your friends. Use these questions to help you.

1 Have you got a favourite friend? Tell the class about him/her.

2 How often do you see him/her?

3 Does he/she go to the same school as you?

4 What do you like doing with your friends?

3 CHARACTERS

Use the words from the box to describe the characters from the story.

> a lady   handsome   kind   jealous   beautiful
> rich   a gentleman   poor

Bentley Dummle

Estella

....

....

....

....

....

....

Pip

Biddy

....

....

....

....

....

....

4 WHO DID IT?

Complete the following questions with the past simple of the verb in brackets. Then say which character (A-E) did it.

WHO...

1 ☐ .... (*steal*) some food from his sister?
2 ☐ .... (*take*) Pip to visit Miss Havisham?
3 ☐ .... (*fight*) with Pip in the garden at Satis House?
4 ☐ .... (*learn*) to be a gentleman?
5 ☐ .... (*meet*) Pip again in London?
6 ☐ .... (*write*) a letter to Mr Drummle?
7 ☐ .... (*teach*) Estella to hate men?
8 ☐ .... (*buy*) new clothes and new furniture?

A Pip's uncle   B Pip   C Estella   D Miss Havisham   E Herbert

5 NOTICES

Which notice (A-H) says this (1-5)? There is an example at the beginning (0).

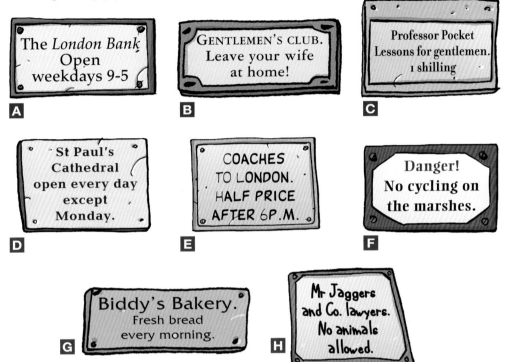

A
The *London Bank*
Open
weekdays 9-5

B
GENTLEMEN'S CLUB.
Leave your wife
at home!

C
Professor Pocket
Lessons for gentlemen.
1 shilling

D
St Paul's
Cathedral
open every day
except
Monday.

E
COACHES
TO LONDON.
HALF PRICE
AFTER 6P.M.

F
Danger!
No cycling on
the marshes.

G
Biddy's Bakery.
Fresh bread
every morning.

H
Mr Jaggers
and Co. lawyers.
No animals
allowed.

0   ...D... You can visit this place from Tuesday to Sunday.

1   .... You can't ride your bike here.

2   .... It is more expensive to travel in the morning.

3   .... Leave your dog outside.

4   .... You can't get money at the weekend.

5   .... Women can't come in here.

BEFORE YOU READ

1 READING PICTURES

Look at the picture on page 45 and answer these questions.

1   Describe the man.

2   Who do you think this man is?

CHAPTER SIX

The Visitor

One night, Pip was studying at home. It was a dark night and there was a storm outside. He could hear the wind and the rain in the London streets. Suddenly, somebody arrived at the door. It was an old man.

Pip: No, I don't. Please go away.

Magwitch: But I know you. You're my gentleman.

Pip: This is a mistake.

Magwitch: No, there's no mistake. You're a gentleman because you've got my money! You're my gentleman.

The man talked to Pip about the past.

> Do you remember the marshes? Do you remember the churchyard? Do you remember the prisoner? Well, I'm that prisoner. My name is Abel Magwitch.

> But... it's impossible!

Magwitch: No, dear boy. You helped me. I remember the food and the file. I was a prisoner in Australia, but now I've got a sheep farm there. I've got a lot of money. Jaggers is my lawyer. He gives you money from me, dear boy! I'm in England to see you.

Pip: I don't understand. Miss Havisham is my benefactor.

Magwitch: No, no. You're wrong. I'm your benefactor.

Pip: This is terrible. I can't take your money. I can't marry Estella. I hate you!

45

Now, Pip knew the truth. [1] He told his friends everything.

> Magwitch must go back to Australia.

> It's dangerous for Abel, Pip. The police are looking for him. We must help him.

Pip: It's the end of my dreams. I'm poor again.

Wemmick: Abel Magwitch must hide [2] from the police. His enemy is looking for him.

Magwitch: I'm happy with you, Pip. You're like a son to me. I don't want to go back to Australia.

1. **the truth** : the real situation.
2. **hide** : go to a place where no one can find him. Past simple = hid.

Pip decided to help Magwitch. They had to go to Australia together. But first he wanted to see Joe and Biddy again. He went back to their village in the country.

Biddy: Goodbye? Where are you going?

Pip: I'm going to Australia. I can't tell you any more. But thank you both for everything. You're my best friends.

UNDERSTANDING THE TEXT

1 COMPREHENSION CHECK

Read these sentences about Chapter Six. Choose the correct answer (A, B or C). There is an example at the beginning (0).

0	Pip was	A drinking.
		(B) studying.
		C dancing.
1	The man arrived on a	A dark, wet night.
		B fine night.
		C light, windy night.
2	Pip	A recognised the visitor.
		B didn't recognise the visitor.
		C remembered the name of the visitor.
3	The visitor was	A the prisoner's enemy.
		B the prisoner.
		C Pip's father.
4	The money came from	A his family.
		B sheep-farming.
		C selling diamonds.
5	The prisoner was very	A poor.
		B ill.
		C rich.
6	Abel Magwitch was	A Pip's benefactor.
		B Pip's lawyer.
		C an Australian uncle.
7	Pip	A wanted to keep the money.
		B didn't want to keep the money.
		C decided to spend the money.
8	It was	A lucky for Magwitch in England.
		B safe for Magwitch in England.
		C dangerous for Magwitch in England.

2 VOCABULARY

Read the definitions of words from Chapter Six. What is the word for each one? The first letter is already there. There is one space for each other letter in the word. There is an example at the beginning (0).

0   Jaggers gave a lot of this to Pip.   m o n e y

1   Hopes for the future.   d_ _ _ _ _

2   Something that you do or think which is wrong.   m_ _ _ _ _ _

3   These people help us if there is a crime.   p_ _ _ _ _

4   We eat this.   f_ _ _

5   These are the people who you talk to and spend
    time with.   f_ _ _ _ _

3 WRITING

Read this note from Pip to Estella.

*I'm happy that you are in London. Where are you staying?
Can I visit you?
Do you want to go to the theatre with me?
Write back soon.
Pip*

Here is Estella's answer. Put the parts of the note in the right order. There is an example at the beginning (0).

A   Dear Pip,

B   First let me tell you my address.

C   Please come and see me tomorrow.

D   But we can go to Lady Brackley's dance.

E   Thank you for writing to me.

F   It's 17 Charlotte Street.

G   I don't like the theatre.

H   PS Charlotte Street is in Richmond.

I   See you tomorrow.

0 ...A...   1 ....   2 ....   3 ....   4 ....   5 ....   6 ....   7 ....   8 ....

4 VOCABULARY – WEATHER

Look at these different weather adjectives and label each picture with the correct word from the box.

windy   rainy   stormy   snowy   cloudy   sunny

| 1 | 2 | 3 | 4 | 5 | 6 |

T: GRADE 3

5 SPEAKING: WEATHER

When Magwitch arrived at Pip's house, there was a storm outside. Talk about the weather. Use these questions to help you.

1 What is the weather like today?
2 What was the weather like yesterday?
3 What is your favourite type of weather? Why?
4 What is the weather usually like on your birthday?

BEFORE YOU READ

1 LISTENING

Listen to the first part of Chapter Seven. Are these sentences true (T) or false (F). Correct the false sentences.

	T	F
1 Pip, Miss Havisham, Estella and Bentley Drummle were all at Satis House.	☐	☐
2 Pip didn't have much money now.	☐	☐
3 Estella loved Pip.	☐	☐
4 Estella was married.	☐	☐

2 WHAT HAPPENS NEXT?

Talk about the following questions with your class.

1 Do you think Estella will marry Bentley Drummle?
2 Does Estella love him?

50

CHAPTER SEVEN

Fire!

Pip wanted to see Miss Havisham again, so he went to Satis  House. Estella was there with Miss Havisham.

Miss Havisham: I'm sorry, Pip.

Pip: Estella, marry me. I'm poor again, but I love you.

Estella: No, Pip. I can't marry you. I want to marry Bentley Drummle!

Pip and Miss Havisham were surprised and angry.

> I don't know anything about this. I can't believe it!

> It's true, Miss Havisham. I want to be Mrs Bentley Drummle. Forget me, Pip!

Miss Havisham: But I gave you my money, my jewels and my love! I don't want you to marry a man. I hate all men. I want you here with me. Do you love me, Estella?

Estella: No, Miss Havisham. I can't love. I haven't got a heart. That was your lesson to me. Goodbye, Pip.

Pip: This is your fault, [1] Miss Havisham. Estella hasn't got a heart because you taught her to hate men. She doesn't love Drummle. He's rich and handsome, but he's cruel. It will be a terrible marriage. Goodbye!

Pip left Satis House and went back to London. There, someone gave Pip a letter from Wemmick. It said, 'DON'T GO HOME!' Pip went to see Wemmick.

1. **This is your fault** : It happened because of you.

Pip agreed. But Miss Havisham wanted to see him again. He went back to Satis House.

Miss Havisham: You're sad. And now Estella is married to a terrible man. It's my fault. Do you forgive me?

Pip: Yes, I forgive you.

Miss Havisham: I want to help you, Pip. I want to give you some money. I have got a heart.

Pip: Thank you. But nobody can help me. I want Estella.

Miss Havisham was sitting very near the fire. Suddenly, her old wedding dress began to burn! Pip saved her, but the old clothes burnt quickly. She was very ill.

He waited for the doctor. He was thinking, 'I want to see Joe and Biddy. They really love me. But I haven't got any time. I must go back to London. Abel Magwitch must escape.' [1]

1. **escape** : go away from his enemies.

UNDERSTANDING THE TEXT

1 **COMPREHENSION CHECK**
Complete the sentences (1-8) with the correct endings (A-H).

1 ☐ Pip visited
2 ☐ Pip
3 ☐ Estella couldn't
4 ☐ Pip and Miss Havisham were
5 ☐ Pip thought Drummle
6 ☐ Wemmick
7 ☐ Magwitch had to escape from
8 ☐ Herbert's friend, Clara, lived

A with her father.
B was a terrible husband for Estella.
C knew that Miss Havisham was not his benefactor.
D sent Pip a message.
E marry Pip.
F Miss Havisham.
G his enemies.
H surprised by Estella's news.

2 **WHO DID IT?**
Which character (A-G) did these things (1-6)? There is an example at the beginning (0).

A Pip
B Estella
C Miss Havisham
D Wemmick
E Herbert
F Clara and her father
G Bentley Drummle

WHO...

0 ☐G☐ did Estella want to marry?
1 ☐ had a friend who lived near the river?
2 ☐ said that she had a heart?
3 ☐ had Miss Havisham's money and jewels?
4 ☐ tried to save Miss Havisham?
5 ☐ did Magwitch stay with?
6 ☐ helped Pip and Herbert with the escape plans?

'I MUST GO BACK TO LONDON.'

To is a preposition. We use prepositions to show place, time or method.

3 PREPOSITIONS

A   **Fill in the gaps in these sentences from Chapter Seven using the prepositions in the box.**

near   for   about (x2)   from   with   to   in

1 ☐ You don't care .... me.
2 ☐ I don't know anything .... this.
3 ☐ I want you here .... me.
4 ☐ Abel must hide .... them.
5 ☐ They know he's .... London.
6 ☐ They live .... the river.
7 ☐ And now Estella is married .... a terrible man.
8 ☐ He waited .... the doctor.

B   **Which character (A-D) said or did the things in sentences 1-8?**

A Wemmick   B Pip   C Herbert   D Miss Havisham

KET

4 WRITING
Read this e-mail from your friend, Alison.

Dear Tom,
Would you like to go to a party tonight? The party is at the Lion Hotel and it starts at 9.00. What do you want to take to the party? What time can we meet?
Do you want to go by taxi or bus?
Let me know soon,
Alison

Write Alison an e-mail. Answer her questions.
Write 25-35 words.

BEFORE YOU READ

1 LISTENING

Listen to the first part of Chapter Eight. For questions 1-6, tick (✓) A, B or C. There is an example at the beginning (0).

0 Pip and Herbert were with
   A Estella.
   Ⓑ Wemmick.
   C Magwitch.

1 Magwitch had to leave London
   A by boat.
   B at night.
   C by train.

2 He had to take the ship to
   A Australia.
   B France.
   C Hamburg.

3 Everyday, Pip and Herbert
   A rowed on the Thames.
   B swam in the river.
   C went on a ship to Hamburg.

4 Magwitch wanted to be
   A alone.
   B with Pip.
   C with Herbert.

5 Where did they hide?
   A In Ireland.
   B On an island.
   C On a ship.

6 In the other boat there were
   A three people.
   B five people.
   C four people.

2 READING PICTURES
Look at the picture on page 59 and answer these questions.

1 Who is in the boat?
2 What are they doing?
3 What do you think will happen next?

CHAPTER EIGHT

The Escape

Magwitch had to go back to Australia. Wemmick helped Pip and Herbert. They made a plan.

Wemmick: Row [1] on the river every day. Do the same thing every day. But one day, take Magwitch with you. Row to the end of the Thames where it meets the sea. Catch the big ship to Hamburg. Then go to Australia. Magwitch will be safe there.

Pip and Herbert: Good idea! Let's do it!

1. **Row** : use oars to move a boat.

One night, Pip and Herbert took their boat to meet Magwitch. He was wearing a disguise. [1] They rowed towards the sea at the end of the River Thames.

Magwitch: I'm very happy, Pip. You're my son now. I want to be with you.

Herbert: Shh! I think that someone is following us. We must be careful. The police mustn't catch Magwitch in England.

They continued to go down the river. They hid on an island during the night. In the morning, they looked for the big ship.

1. **disguise** : something you wear or use so that people do not know who you are.

They saw the ship. But there was another boat. There were three policemen in it and another man.

Policeman: Stop! That man is a prisoner from Australia. You mustn't help him. Stop!

Pip: Row faster! Faster! We must catch the ship.

Magwitch: Who's that man in the boat with the police? I think I know him. Yes – it's my enemy, Compeyson!

The man in the other boat was Compeyson. He was the other prisoner from the marshes. He was helping the police because he hated Magwitch. And Magwitch hated him.

Pip and Herbert rowed quickly towards the ship. But the police were near, now. Magwitch was very angry. He hated Compeyson.

He jumped into the other boat and fought Compeyson. They

fell into the water. The big ship passed over them. Pip jumped into the sea to rescue [1] Magwitch.

> We arrest you, Abel Magwitch! But where is Compeyson?

> He's dead. He went under the ship. His body is in the water.

Police: Come with us. We're going back to London. We're going to take Magwitch to prison. He must die!

Pip: No! He's like a father to me! Please, don't take him!

1. **rescue** : to help.

UNDERSTANDING THE TEXT

KET

1 COMPREHENSION CHECK

Are these sentences 'Right' (A) or 'Wrong' (B)? If there is not enough information to answer 'Right' (A) or 'Wrong' (B), choose 'Doesn't say' (C). There is an example at the beginning (0).

0   Magwitch didn't want people to know who he was.
   Ⓐ Right   B Wrong   C Doesn't say

1   Magwitch wanted to catch the ship to Hamburg.
   A Right   B Wrong   C Doesn't say

2   Magwitch didn't want Pip to come with him to Australia.
   A Right   B Wrong   C Doesn't say

3   Pip and Herbert were afraid when they were escaping with Magwitch.
   A Right   B Wrong   C Doesn't say

4   There were three policemen on the big ship.
   A Right   B Wrong   C Doesn't say

5   Compeyson saw Magwitch in the boat and told the police.
   A Right   B Wrong   C Doesn't say

6   Magwitch recognised Compeyson because of his scar.
   A Right   B Wrong   C Doesn't say

7   Magwitch jumped into the water and swam towards the big ship.
   A Right   B Wrong   C Doesn't say

8   They looked for Compeyson's body.
   A Right   B Wrong   C Doesn't say

KET

2 FILL IN THE GAPS

Complete this information about the River Thames. Write ONE word for each space. There is an example at the beginning (0).

(0) ......The....... Thames is a very long river. (1) .... are many bridges which cross the Thames. Today, you can (2) .... many famous places if you travel down the Thames (3) .... boat. (4) .... example, there are the Houses of Parliament, the London Eye and Cleopatra's Needle.
Near the end (5) .... the river, you can see the Thames Barrier. This is (6) .... important for London (7) .... it controls the water from the sea which can enter the river and cover the city. After London, the river joins (8) .... sea. This is where Pip (9) .... Magwitch want to catch the (10) .... to Hamburg.

'I THINK THAT SOMEONE IS FOLLOWING US.'

We use the present continuous of verbs to describe things which are happening at this moment. We make the present continuous by adding **ing** to the infinitive of the verb.

*You **are reading** this book.*

3 PRESENT CONTINUOUS

A   **What are they doing? Write what the people in the pictures are doing.**

....

....

B   **You are one of the passengers on the ship to Hamburg and you are describing what you can see. Complete these sentences with the present continuous of these verbs. There is an example at the beginning (0).**

> arrest   call   come   fall   fight   go (x 2)   happen
> jump   pass   pull   row   sit   slow   not stop

Look, there is a boat! The men (0) ...*are rowing*..... very fast. Look! Another boat (1) .... from the island. Three policemen (2) .... in it with another man. The policemen (3) .... to the other boat but they (4) .... Our ship (5) .... down but we are already very near them. Look! Two of the men (6) .... They (7) .... into the river. Another man (8) .... into the water after them. Where are they? Our ship (9) .... over them. What (10) .... ? They (11) .... two of the men back into the boat. The policemen (12) .... them. Where is the other man? Is he dead? It's too late now. Our ship (13) .... fast again. We (14) .... to Hamburg. Goodbye, England!

Read the information about Abel Magwitch and complete the police record below. There is an example at the beginning (0).

WANTED

Do you know this man?

His name is Abel Magwitch and he
is about sixty years old.
He has got long grey hair and
dark eyes. He is tall and strong.
He escaped from prison in
London, eighteen years ago and
the police want to catch him.
If you see this man,
do not talk to him.

Call Cheapside Police on 6523.

THE PRISONER

0   Name: ....Abel Magwitch..

1   Age: ....

2   Hair colour: ....

3   Physical description: ....

4   History: ....

5   What to do: ....

BEFORE YOU READ

1 **LISTENING**

Listen to the first part of Chapter Nine. Are these sentences true (T) or false (F)? Correct the false sentences.

		T	F
1	Magwitch went back to London with the police.	☐	☐
2	The police wanted to ask Magwitch some questions.	☐	☐
3	Pip saw Magwitch in prison.	☐	☐
4	Pip was very happy because he loved Estella.	☐	☐
5	Pip had to work for the shopkeepers.	☐	☐

Transportation to Australia

THE CONVICT SHIP.

A convict ship leaves for Australia. The criminals were also called 'convicts'. Friends and family wave goodbye: probably they will not meet again.

In the 18th and 19th centuries a lot of people moved from the country to the cities and, because of this, there was more crime. The punishment [1] for many crimes was hanging: [2] this was the punishment for stealing things, as well as for killing people.

There were very many criminals, and to hang so many criminals was cruel. But there weren't enough prisons for all the criminals. The government even had to use old ships as prisons, as you saw in Chapter One.

So, the government started sending criminals to other countries, first to America and then to Australia. The name for this was 'transportation': criminals left Britain, and they could help to build a new country.

Some of the criminals were dangerous: they had to stay in Australia for life. But some of them did very small things: a girl stole something from a shop – she went to Australia for seven years!

It was 15,000 miles to Australia, and the journey there by ship was

1. **punishment** : what the government does to a criminal.
2. **hanging:** the criminal is killed with a rope around his neck.

A warder watches prisoners on a prison ship. This ship had space for 600 prisoners. Prisoners stayed here before transportation on a convict ship.

about 100 days. There wasn't much fresh air inside the ships, and a lot of the prisoners became ill and died. Between 1787 and 1868, 162,000 prisoners – about a fifth of them women – went from Britain to Australia.

The first eleven ships arrived at Botany Bay, in New South Wales, on 20 January 1788. After a few days they moved to Port Jackson, which became the first permanent European colony in Australia. This area became the city of Sydney, and the day they arrived there, 26 January 1788, is now 'Australia Day'.

The prisoners had to work hard: they helped to build new towns. Sometimes they became free men and women after a few years, and they became honest, hard-working members of society.

But serious criminals could not go back to England. If they did, and the police caught them, the punishment was hanging.

1 COMPREHENSION CHECK
Answer the following questions.

1 What were the reasons for transportation?
2 What do these numbers refer to? a)100   b) 15,000   c) 162,000
3 What happened to the convicts in Australia?

CHAPTER NINE

Joe to the Rescue

The police took Pip and Magwitch back to London.

The police wanted to hang Magwitch. They said he was a criminal. But Magwitch was very ill – he was dying. Pip went to visit him in prison.

Abel, I haven't got a father, so you are my father now.

My dear boy, I love you. You're my fine gentleman. Are you happy?

Pip: I can't be happy. I love a beautiful woman. Her name is Estella. But she's the wife of another man.

Magwitch: I hope you will be happy soon, Pip. Goodbye, I'm dying...

Abel Magwitch died. Pip was very sad. He didn't have any friends in London because Herbert was working in another country. Pip also had problems with money. He had to pay some shopkeepers, [1] but he didn't have enough money. The shopkeepers were very angry with him and asked the police to arrest him.

Pip was very ill. He was dreaming about when he was a child. He was dreaming about Joe, his best friend. Then he woke up. Joe was there!

Come home with me, Pip. I've got enough money to pay the shopkeepers. You're free.

But you're poor, Joe.

Joe: Money isn't important. You're important because Biddy and I love you.

1. **shopkeepers** : people who have got shops and sell things.

Pip went back to the country and lived in the village again. He got better and he began to think about love.

He thought, 'I love Estella. But she's cruel and she hasn't got a heart. Biddy is a very good person. She loves me.'

Pip wanted to ask Biddy to marry him. But there was something he did not know.

Pip: But... Well, that's wonderful news! You're my best friends. I'm very happy for you both!

UNDERSTANDING THE TEXT

1 COMPREHENSION CHECK
Complete the sentences (1-10) with the correct endings (A-J).

1 ☐ Magwitch had to	A any friends in London.
2 ☐ Pip	B were very angry with Pip.
3 ☐ Magwitch didn't have	C he loved Pip.
4 ☐ Pip didn't have	D different from Estella.
5 ☐ The shopkeepers	E wear chains.
6 ☐ Pip was	F marry Biddy.
7 ☐ Joe paid the money because	G visited Magwitch in prison.
8 ☐ Biddy was	H married Joe.
9 ☐ Pip wanted to	I a long time to live.
10 ☐ Biddy	J dreaming.

KET

2 WRITING
Complete this letter to Herbert. Write ONE word for each space. There is an example at the beginning (0).

Dear Herbert,

Joe and Biddy (0) ..are......... getting married. I (1) .... very happy. They are (2) .... happy together. They are both kind and gentle people.

I am still in love (3) .... Estella. I know that she hasn't (4) .... a heart and that she is Drummle's (5) .... , but I can (6) .... forget her. I want to go to Australia (7) .... Africa.

(8) .... you and Clara getting married?

Write to me soon.

Your friend,

Pip

3 WHAT DO YOU THINK?
Joe said that money isn't important.

1 Do you agree with Joe?
2 What is more important than money in your life?

4 WORD GAME: IRREGULAR VERBS IN THE PAST

A Complete this crossword with the past tense of the following verbs from the story.

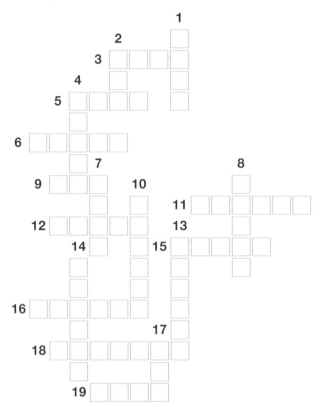

ACROSS	DOWN
3 wake	1 fall
5 sing	2 win
6 steal	4 speak
9 meet	7 take
11 teach	8 burn
12 write	10 learn
15 find	13 fight
16 catch	14 buy
18 think	17 hide
19 pay	

B Can you find five verbs in the crossword which sound the same?

CHAPTER TEN

Estella

So, Pip began to think about Estella again. There was some  news from London. Bentley Drummle was a very bad husband: he hit Estella. She never went out. People said that she was very unhappy.

> Poor Estella. She's learning to have a heart!

> You're very sad, Pip. Can we help you?

Pip: No, my friends. I must leave England. I want to go to Africa or Australia. I want to work hard and forget my problems.

Pip left England and went to the East. He worked hard and tried to forget everything in the past. After eleven years, he came back. He went to see Joe and Biddy and their child. Their son's name was Pip! Pip decided to visit Satis House for the last time. Miss Havisham was dead. The house was not there; there were only ruins. [1] It was a grey day and he walked in the garden.

Pip: But wait. There's someone in the garden. I can see a woman. She's coming towards me. Who is it?

1. **ruins :**

Estella walked through the garden and saw Pip. She was still very beautiful, but her face was sad.

Estella! Why are you here?

Bentley Drummle is dead. There was an accident with his horse. I'm here to say goodbye to Satis House.

Pip: And have you got a heart now?
Estella: Yes, Pip, I have. But it's too late...

Pip was very happy. They talked for a long time in the garden and they held hands. They were not young and free and they had a lot of problems, but they went out of the garden together.

Pip knew the meaning of his life now. Money wasn't important. Being a gentleman wasn't important. Great expectations weren't important. Friends were important. He and Estella were friends now. He knew that this was not the last goodbye between Estella and himself.

UNDERSTANDING THE TEXT

KET

1 COMPREHENSION CHECK

Read this summary of Chapter Ten. Choose the best word (A, B or C) for each space.

Pip often thought (**1**) .... Estella. He heard some news from London. Estella (**2**) .... not have a good marriage and she was not happy. Pip was sad too and he felt sorry for Estella.
Pip decided to go (**3**) .... the East to work hard and forget (**4**) .... problems. He stayed there for more (**5**) .... ten years. While Pip was away, Joe and Biddy had a child (**6**) .... they called Pip.
When Pip came (**7**) .... to England, he went to Satis House. While he (**8**) .... thinking about when he was a boy, he met Estella in the garden. (**9**) .... husband, Bentley Drummle, was dead and Estella was different. Now she had a heart. Pip understood that friends were (**10**) .... important than money.

1	A to	B about	C on
2	A did	B didn't	C was
3	A to	B for	C at
4	A it	B his	C their
5	A that	B of	C than
6	A who	B why	C where
7	A return	B back	C for
8	A was	B were	C wasn't
9	A His	B Hers	C Her
10	A much	B most	C more

2 ODD ONE OUT

Circle the word which is different from the others in each group.

1	son	sister	husband	uncle
2	garden	flat	house	apartment
3	car	bicycle	train	horse
4	Africa	Australia	England	Asia
5	hand	heart	leg	face

3 FILL IN THE GAPS

Now use the words from exercise 2 to complete these sentences.

1   Pip's .... was often unkind to him.
2   Pip came back to .... after eleven years in the East.
3   Miss Havisham taught Estella not to have a ....
4   Pip and Estella met in the .... at Satis House.
5   Bentley Drummle fell off his ....

4 CONVERSATIONS

**Complete the five conversations. For questions 1-5, choose A, B or C.
There is an example at the beginning (0).**

0   What would you like?

    A   Yes, I would.
    B   I like coffee.
    (C) Tea, please.

1   Is Estella at Satis House?

    A   Yes, she is.
    B   She does.
    C   Yes, she's.

2   What's the time?

    A   At five o'clock.
    B   Half past seven.
    C   Ten minutes.

3   Do you like travelling by coach?

    A   No, I don't.
    B   Yes, it does.
    C   Yes, I like.

4   How old are you?

    A   I have eleven years.
    B   I am ten years.
    C   I am twelve.

5   Is this your house?

    A   No, it's hers.
    B   Yes, it's my.
    C   My house.

PICTURE SUMMARY

Look at the pictures from the story and put them in the correct order.
Use the pictures to tell the story of *Great Expectations*.

EXIT TEST

1 **COMPREHENSION CHECK**
**Complete this summary of Chapters One to Five of *Great Expectations*.
Write ONE word for each space.**

When Pip was young he met a prisoner who asked (1) .... some
food and a file. While he was on the marshes he saw another prisoner.
Then the soldiers caught the prisoners and they both went
(2) .... to prison.
Pip met a young girl (3) .... Estella at Miss Havisham's house.
Pip began to love Estella, but she did (4) .... love him. One day,
while he was in the garden, he met and fought with another boy.
(5) .... name was Herbert.
Pip worked with Joe. His sister was ill and (6) .... kind woman
helped Joe. Her name was Biddy. One day, a gentleman came to the
village and asked (7) .... Pip. He told Pip that he had great
expectations.
Pip had a lot (8) .... money and wanted to know who his
benefactor was, but the gentleman, Mr Jaggers, didn't tell him.
Pip went to live (9) .... London and met Herbert Pocket again.
Pip learnt to be a gentleman. He didn't want (10) .... be friends
with Joe any more. But, now that he was a gentleman, he wanted to
marry Estella.
Estella (11) .... back from Paris, now she was a lady. Pip went
to Satis House to visit Miss Havisham. He thought that (12) ....
was his benefactor.
Estella went to London. She knew a lot of men and Pip was jealous
because she didn't love (13) ....
He went to (14) .... sister's funeral and Pip promised to visit
and write to Joe. But Biddy knew that it wasn't true.

2 **WHO SAYS WHAT?**
**Match each sentence (1-13) from Chapters Six to Ten with a character
(A-H). You can use the characters more than once.**

1 ☐ 'I want to work hard and forget my problems.'
2 ☐ 'I can't be happy. I love a beautiful woman.'
3 ☐ 'You're my gentleman.'
4 ☐ 'You're free.'
5 ☐ 'It's my enemy, Compeyson.'
6 ☐ 'I'm not a gentleman now, Joe.'

7 ☐ 'I have got a heart.'

8 ☐ 'Row to the end of the Thames where it meets the sea.'

9 ☐ 'But I gave you my money, my jewels and my love.'

10 ☐ 'You mustn't help him. Stop!'

11 ☐ 'I'm here to say goodbye to Satis House.'

12 ☐ 'Pip, I've got some wonderful news!'

13 ☐ 'You don't care about me.'

A Miss Havisham   D Estella   G Joe
B the policeman   E Mr Wemmick   H Biddy
C Pip   F Abel Magwitch

3 ADJECTIVES

Look at these adjectives from the story. Which do you associate with the 'ladies' and 'gentlemen' in the story and which do you associate with the other characters?

kind   rich   good   cruel   happy   proud
handsome   beautiful   poor   unkind

Ladies and Gentlemen ....

....

....

Other characters ....

....

....

Great Expectations

ACT ONE

The Prisoner on the Marshes

Pip was a young boy who didn't have a mother or father. He lived on the marshes, near the great River Thames. One day he was sitting in the churchyard. He was looking at his parents' graves. Suddenly someone came close to him. It was a prisoner. He was escaping from the prison ships on the river. Pip was very afraid.

PRISONER: What's your name?

PIP: P-P-Pip, sir.

PRISONER: I want food. Get me some.

PIP: Y-y-yes, sir. Are you very hungry, sir?

PRISONER: Yes, I am. And bring me a file. I want to cut these chains. But don't tell anyone!

PIP: No, sir!

pause

PIP: How can I get food for the prisoner? Joe is kind but my sister is often angry.

SISTER'S VOICE: You are a bad boy!

PRISONER'S VOICE: Get me some food!

PIP: I'm afraid of my sister. But I'm very afraid of the prisoner. It is very bad to steal food. But I must do it. Where is Joe's file? I must take it to help the prisoner.

Pip got up early and ran across the marshes. It was very cold and grey but the sun was coming up. He saw another prisoner, who ran away. Pip took the food and the file to the prisoner in the churchyard.

PIP: Here's the food. I hope you are not too cold and hungry, sir.

PRISONER: Thank you, boy. This food is good.

PIP: There's another prisoner on the marshes, sir. He's got a scar on his face.

PRISONER: What! He's my enemy! Give me the file. Quick! I must find him.

pause

SISTER (*angrily*): Where is the food for dinner? Pip, do you know?

PIP: N-n-no, sister.

(*knocking at the door*)

JOE: Who is it?

PIP: There are some soldiers at the door.

SISTER: Goodness! What do they want?

SOLDIER: We are looking for two prisoners. They are out on the marshes. Are you Mr Gargery, the blacksmith?

JOE: Yes, sir.

SOLDIER: We want you to repair these handcuffs.

JOE: Yes, sir.

pause

JOE: Here are your handcuffs.

SOLDIER: Thank you, blacksmith. Now we must find the prisoners.

JOE: Can we come with you to the marshes?

SOLDIER: Yes, Mr Gargery.

JOE: Come with me, Pip.

PIP: Y-y-yes, Joe.

pause

JOE: Look, Pip! The prisoners are fighting.

PIP: I don't want to look, Joe.

JOE: Look, Pip! The soldiers are taking the prisoners to the prison ship. Poor men! I feel sorry for them.

Pip (*to himself*): I'm afraid. The prisoner thinks that I'm helping the soldiers. It isn't true!

FIRST PRISONER: You're my enemy. I want to kill you.

SECOND PRISONER: You're stupid. Now we're both going back to prison.

Miss Havisham

A strange, old lady lived in a big house in the village. Her name was Miss Havisham. One day, she asked to see Pip. So Pip's uncle had to take Pip to her house.

SISTER: Miss Havisham is very rich. She's got a lot of money and jewels. You must be good when you're with her, Pip. Perhaps she wants to give you a lot of money.

JOE: Good luck, Pip. Be careful. Some people say Miss Havisham is mad.

Pip's uncle, Mr Pumblechook, took Pip to her house. It was called Satis House. A beautiful, young girl opened the gate for Pip.

ESTELLA (*proudly*): Come in, boy! Miss Havisham wants to see you. But I don't like you. Your boots are dirty and your hands are rough.

PIP: Is Miss Havisham your mother?

ESTELLA: No, I haven't got a mother or father. I live with Miss Havisham and she gives me everything. But don't ask questions, boy!

PIP (*to himself*): The room is very dark. What a strange lady! She is wearing a very old, yellow wedding dress. And all the clocks say the same time: twenty to nine.

MISS HAVISHAM: Hello, Pip. Well, Estella, do you like Pip?

ESTELLA: No, he isn't a gentleman. He's a blacksmith's boy.

MISS HAVISHAM: And Pip, do you like Estella?

PIP: She's very beautiful.

MISS HAVISHAM: Pip thinks you are beautiful, Estella. So break his heart!

Pip often visited Miss Havisham and Estella. Sometimes, they played cards and sometimes, they sang. But Estella was always proud. Pip

84

began to love her, but she didn't love him. One day Miss Havisham took him into a special room. There was a long table with a very old wedding cake on it. There were spiders and mice everywhere.

MISS HAVISHAM: Today is my birthday, Pip. Push me around the table. This is my wedding cake from a long time ago.

PIP (*to himself*): But where is her husband?

MISS HAVISHAM: I hate men. I'm teaching Estella to hate men too, Pip. You are only a boy. But when you are a man, you must leave Satis House for ever.

PIP: But I want to marry Estella.

ESTELLA: Silly boy! I hate you!

Pip met another boy in the garden.

HERBERT: Let's fight. I'm very strong.

PIP: I don't want to fight. It's stupid.

HERBERT: No it isn't. Fighting is the sport of gentlemen.

Pip hit Herbert and he fell down. He got up and Pip hit him again. He fell down. He got up and Pip hit him a third time. He fell down again.

HERBERT: You're the winner.

ESTELLA: Well done, Pip. You can kiss me if you want.

Pip kissed Estella on the cheek.

ESTELLA: Now Miss Havisham wants to say goodbye to you.

MISS HAVISHAM: This is the last time, Pip. I don't want to see you again. Here's some money. You must be a blacksmith.

PIP: But I want to see Estella again. I love her!

MISS HAVISHAM: I'm sending Estella to Paris. She'll become a lady. But you're a blacksmith, Pip. You must work with Joe Gargery.

ACT THREE

The Money

Pip worked with Joe. He loved Joe and Joe loved him but Pip was unhappy because he wasn't a gentleman. He was eighteen years old now. *When Pip's sister was ill, a young woman came to help Joe. Her name was Biddy. She was kind and she was very pretty. She liked Pip very much but Pip couldn't forget Estella.*

PIP: I want to be a gentleman, Biddy. I want to marry Estella. I want to live in London.

BIDDY: I'm happy here with you and Joe, Pip. Joe isn't a gentleman, but he's a very good man.

PIP: Yes, you're right. But...

BIDDY: And the marshes are beautiful. I'm not a lady and I'm not rich, but I like my life.

JOE: Pip! Pip! There's a visitor for you. It's a gentleman from London.

JAGGERS: Is your name Pip?

PIP: Yes, sir.

JAGGERS: I'm Mr Jaggers, a lawyer. I've got some news for you. You're rich. You've got great expectations.

PIP: What! I don't understand...

JAGGERS: Someone wants to give you a lot of money. You must go to London. You must learn to be a gentleman.

PIP: Who is my benefactor, sir?

JAGGERS: I can't tell you the name.

PIP: Is it a man or a woman?

JAGGERS: I can't tell you. Don't ask any more questions. Take this money and buy some gentleman's clothes.

PIP *(thinks)*: Miss Havisham is my benefactor. She wants me to be a gentleman. She wants Estella to be a lady. She wants us to get married. I'm very happy.

ACT FOUR

London

Pip went to London by coach. He saw a big city for the first time. He forgot Joe and Biddy. He only thought about Estella. He went to live in a house in the centre of London, near Mr Jaggers. In the same house, he met Herbert Pocket.

HERBERT: Hello. My name's Herbert.

PIP: Hello. I'm Pip. I remember you! You're the boy from Miss Havisham's garden!

HERBERT: Yes, now I remember you too! But we can be friends now. I want to show you London. My father is a teacher. He can help you to be a gentleman.

PIP: Then I can marry Estella.

HERBERT: Be careful, Pip. Miss Havisham hates men. Many years ago, she was in love. But, on the day of her wedding, the man didn't come to the church. The time was twenty to nine! Estella hates men too.

Pip learnt to be a gentleman. He learnt to speak like a gentleman. He learnt to eat like a gentleman. Joe visited him in London but he didn't stay long. Pip didn't want to talk to his old friend, the blacksmith. Pip was a snob now.

JOE: You're a fine gentleman now, Pip. You've got fine clothes.

PIP: Thank you, Joe.

JOE: Biddy says hello to you, and hopes you are well.

PIP: Thank you, Joe.

JOE: I'm going back to the village now, Pip. London isn't the right place for me.

PIP: Goodbye, Joe.

JOE: Goodbye, Pip.

PIP: I must see Mr Jaggers. I've got a lot of new clothes and new furniture. I must ask for some more money.

pause

JAGGERS: I've got some money for you, Pip. How much do you want?

PIP: A lot, Mr Jaggers.

JAGGERS: All right, Pip. You're twenty-one years old this year. Your benefactor wants to give you some more money.

PIP: But who is my benefactor? It's Miss Havisham, isn't it?

JAGGERS: I can't tell you.

WEMMICK: Here's your money, sir.

PIP (*to himself*): I'm rich. I'm a gentleman. Now I can marry Estella!

ACT FIVE

Estella in London

Estella came back from Paris. She was a lady and Pip was a gentleman. Pip went to visit Miss Havisham at Satis House and met Estella. Pip thought that Miss Havisham was his benefactor.

MISS HAVISHAM: You're rich now, Pip. But you don't know the name of your benefactor.

PIP: That's true, Miss Havisham. But, I want to thank my benefactor.

MISS HAVISHAM: Good. Look, here is Estella.

PIP: You're very beautiful, Estella.

ESTELLA: Ah, it's the blacksmith's boy. You're a gentleman now! Your shoes are clean!

MISS HAVISHAM: Is she beautiful, Pip?

PIP: Yes, she is.

MISS HAVISHAM: Love her, Pip. Love her, love her, love her!

(*She pauses*) Estella! Break his heart!

Estella came to London. She and Pip were friends but she met and danced with a lot of different men. Pip was jealous. One evening, at a party, he was angry.

PIP: Estella, please don't dance with other men! Don't smile at them! Marry me! I'm a gentleman now, and I love you.

ESTELLA: Don't be silly, Pip. I haven't got a heart. I can't love you. You'll only be unhappy with me.

GENTLEMAN: Do you want to dance, Miss Estella?

ESTELLA: Yes, thank you, sir. Goodbye, Pip.

PIP: What can I do? Herbert tells me to forget Estella. But I love her.

pause

HERBERT: Meet my friends, Pip. Let's drink together.

STUDENT: Let's drink to our lady friends. Drummle, who is your special friend?

DRUMMLE (*raising his glass*): To Estella. The most beautiful woman in London!

PIP: You can't drink to Estella. You don't know her.

DRUMMLE: Why not? I know her well. She's my special friend. I often dance with her.

PIP: You're lying.

HERBERT: Be careful. Everyone's listening.

They met again the following week.

DRUMMLE: Here's a letter from the lady. Everyone can read it.

ESTELLA'S VOICE: 'Yes, I know Mr Drummle. Sometimes, I dance with him. Estella.'

PIP: I'm sorry, Mister Drummle. You're right. You aren't a liar.

DRUMMLE: And you, sir, are not a gentleman.

STUDENTS: Ha ha! Ha ha!

Pip went to see Estella.

PIP: Estella, why do you see Bentley Drummle?

ESTELLA: I know a lot of men, Pip. I'm very beautiful. Miss Havisham gives me a lot of money. They all want to marry me.

PIP: But, Estella, Drummle is a terrible person. He's cruel and stupid.

ESTELLA: I like cruel, stupid, rich men. Remember, Pip, I haven't got a heart.

Biddy wrote a letter to Pip. She told him that Pip's sister, Joe's wife, was dead. Pip went back to the village. After the funeral he spoke to Biddy.

BIDDY: Joe is very sad, Pip. You never write to him or visit us.

PIP: I'm sorry Biddy. But don't worry. I want to visit Joe often now. My sister is dead and he is alone.

BIDDY: But... I can't believe you, Pip. You're a gentleman now and you don't want to remember Joe and me.

PIP: No, Biddy. I remember you all.

BIDDY (*to herself*): It isn't true. Pip only thinks about Satis House. He forgets his real friends.

ACT SIX
The Visitor

One night, Pip was studying at home. It was a dark night and there was a storm outside. Somebody arrived at the door.

PIP: Who are you? What do you want?

MAGWITCH: My boy! My boy! Do you know who I am?

PIP: No, I don't. Please go away.

MAGWITCH: But I know you. You're my gentleman.

PIP: This is a mistake.

MAGWITCH: No, there's no mistake. You're a gentleman because you've got my money! You're my gentleman. Do you remember the marshes? Do you remember the churchyard? Do you remember the prisoner? I'm that prisoner. My name is Abel Magwitch.

PIP: But… it's impossible.

MAGWITCH: No, dear boy. You helped me. I remember the food and the file. I was a prisoner in Australia, but now I've got a sheep farm there. Jaggers is my lawyer. He gives you money from me, dear boy! I'm in England to see you.

PIP: I don't understand. Miss Havisham is my benefactor.

MAGWITCH: No, no. You're wrong. I'm your benefactor.

PIP: This is terrible. I can't take your money. I can't marry Estella. I hate you!

Now, Pip knew the truth. He told his friends everything.

JAGGERS: Magwitch must go back to Australia.

HERBERT: It's dangerous for Abel, Pip. The police are looking for him. We must help him.

PIP: It's the end of my dreams. I'm poor again.

WEMMICK: Abel Magwitch must hide from the police. His enemy is looking for him.

MAGWITCH: I'm happy with you, Pip. You're like a son to me. I don't want to go back to Australia.

PIP: Herbert, I must help Magwitch. We must go to Australia together. First, I want to see Joe and Biddy again.

pause

JOE: Pip! I'm so glad to see you. How are you? How is your life as a gentleman in London?

PIP: I'm not a gentleman now, Joe. It's a long story and I can't tell you everything. But I'm here to say goodbye.

BIDDY: Goodbye? Where are you going?

PIP: I'm going to Australia. I can't tell you any more. But thank you both for everything. You're my best friends.

ACT SEVEN
Fire!

Pip wanted to see Miss Havisham again, so he went to Satis House. Estella was there with Miss Havisham.

MISS HAVISHAM: Pip! Why are you here?

PIP: I know everything. You aren't my benefactor! You don't care about me.

MISS HAVISHAM: I'm sorry, Pip.

PIP: Estella, marry me. I'm poor again, but I love you.

ESTELLA: No, Pip. I can't marry you. I want to marry Bentley Drummle!

PIP AND MISS HAVISHAM: What! What do you mean!

MISS HAVISHAM: Pip, I don't know anything about this. I can't believe it.

ESTELLA: It's true, Miss Havisham. I want to be Mrs Bentley Drummle. Forget me, Pip!

MISS HAVISHAM: But I gave you my money, my jewels and my love! I don't want you to marry a man. I hate all men. I want you here with me. Do you love me, Estella?

ESTELLA: No, Miss Havisham. I can't love. I haven't got a heart. That was your lesson to me. Goodbye, Pip.

PIP: This is your fault, Miss Havisham. Estella hasn't got a heart because you taught her to hate men. She doesn't love Drummle. He's rich and handsome, but he's cruel. It will be a terrible marriage. Goodbye!

Pip left Satis House and went back to London. There, someone gave Pip a letter from Wemmick. It said: 'DON'T GO HOME!' Pip went to see Wemmick.

WEMMICK: Magwitch has got a lot of enemies. They know he's in London. They're following you because they want to find him. Abel must hide from them.

HERBERT: Abel can stay with my friend, Clara, and her father. They live near the river.

Miss Havisham asked him to visit her again. He went back to Satis House.

MISS HAVISHAM: You're sad. And now Estella is married to a terrible man. It's my fault. Do you forgive me?

PIP: Yes, I forgive you.

MISS HAVISHAM: I want to help you, Pip. I want to give you some money. I have got a heart.

PIP: Thank you. But nobody can help me. I want Estella.

MISS HAVISHAM: Don't go, Pip.

PIP (*going*): Goodbye, Miss Havisham.

MISS HAVISHAM: Pip! My dress! The fire! Aaaaaaaaa!

Miss Havisham's dress was burning. Pip saved her but the old clothes burnt quickly. She was very ill.

PIP (*thinks*): Poor Miss Havisham. She hasn't got anything now.

ACT EIGHT
The Escape

Magwitch had to go back to Australia. Wemmick helped Pip and Herbert. They made a plan.

WEMMICK: There's a ship to Hamburg. It leaves from the end of the River Thames. But no one must see you when you leave London.

PIP AND HERBERT: What can we do?

WEMMICK: Row on the river every day. Do the same thing every day. But one day, take Magwitch with you. Row to the end of the Thames where it meets the sea. Catch the big ship to Hamburg. Then go to Australia. Magwitch will be safe there.

PIP AND HERBERT: Good idea! Let's do it!

One night, Pip and Herbert took their boat to meet Magwitch. He was wearing a disguise. They rowed towards the sea at the end of the River Thames.

MAGWITCH: Thank you, Pip, my boy. But I don't want to be alone in Australia.

PIP: Don't worry, Abel. I'm coming with you. There is nothing in England for me. Estella is married.

MAGWITCH: I'm very happy, Pip. You're my son now. I want to be with you.

HERBERT: Shh! I think that someone is following us. We must be careful. The police mustn't catch Magwitch in England.

PIP: There's an island. Let's stop the boat and hide on the island for the night.

HERBERT: Yes, in the morning, you can catch the ship.

MAGWITCH: Thank you, my two fine gentlemen.

pause

HERBERT: Look! There's the ship. Row quickly! We must catch it.

PIP: But what's that? There's a boat behind us.

HERBERT: There are four men in it.

PIP: I can see three policemen. And there's another man.

MAN: That's Magwitch. Abel Magwitch.

POLICEMAN: Stop! That man is a prisoner from Australia. You mustn't help him. Stop!

PIP: Row faster! Faster! We must catch the ship.

ABEL: Who's that man in the boat with the police? I think I know him. Yes – It's my enemy, Compeyson!

MAN: Magwitch, this is the end for you.

MAGWITCH: Compeyson, I hate you.

Pip and Herbert rowed quickly towards the ship. But the police were near now. Magwitch was very angry. He hated Compeyson. He jumped into the other boat and fought Compeyson. They fell into the water. The big ship passed over them. Pip jumped into the sea to rescue Magwitch.

POLICE: We arrest you, Abel Magwitch! But where is Compeyson?

PIP: He's dead. He went under the ship. His body is in the water.

POLICE: Come with us. We're going back to London. We're going to take Magwitch to prison. He must die!

PIP: No! He's like a father to me! Please, don't take him.

MAGWITCH: I'm very cold. The river was very cold. I hurt my head.

PIP: Let me hold you in my arms.

POLICEMAN: Magwitch is our prisoner. He must wear chains.

ACT NINE

Joe to the Rescue

Now, there was a big problem. The police wanted to hang Magwitch. They said he was a criminal. But Magwitch was very ill – he was dying. Pip went to visit him in prison.

PIP: Abel, I haven't got a father, so you are my father now.

MAGWITCH: My dear boy, I love you. You're my fine gentleman. Are you happy?

PIP: I can't be happy. I love a beautiful woman. Her name is Estella.

But she's the wife of another man.

MAGWITCH: I hope you will be happy soon, Pip. Goodbye, I'm dying...

Abel Magwitch died. Pip was very sad. He didn't have any friends in London because Herbert was working in another country. Pip also had problems with money. He had to pay some shopkeepers, but he didn't have enough money. The shopkeepers were very angry with him and asked the police to arrest him. Pip was very ill. He was dreaming about when he was a child. He was dreaming about Joe, his best friend. Then he woke up. Joe was there!

JOE: Come home with me, Pip. I've got enough money to pay the shopkeepers. You're free.

PIP: But you're poor, Joe.

JOE: Money isn't important. You're important because Biddy and I love you.

Pip went back to the country and lived in the village again. He got better and began to think about love.

PIP: I love Estella. But she's cruel and she hasn't got a heart. Biddy is a very good person. She loves me.

PIP: Biddy, I want to...

BIDDY: Pip, I've got some wonderful news. Joe and I are getting married today.

PIP: But... Well, that is wonderful news. You're my best friends. I'm very happy for you both.

ACT TEN

Estella

BIDDY: What's the matter, Pip?

PIP: There is some news from London. Bentley Drummle is a very bad husband: he hits Estella. She never goes out. People say that she is very unhappy.

BIDDY: I'm sorry, Pip.

PIP: Poor Estella. She's learning to have a heart!

JOE AND BIDDY: You're very sad, Pip. Can we help you?

PIP: No, my friends. I must leave England. I want to go to Africa or Australia. I want to work hard and forget my problems.

Pip left England and went to the East. He worked hard and tried to forget everything in the past. After eleven years, he came back.

PIP: Here's the garden of Satis House. I remember when I was a boy here. Estella was a beautiful little girl and I was a poor boy from the blacksmith's family. I remember the house. I remember the clocks... But wait. There's someone in the garden. I can see a woman. She's coming towards me. Who is it?

ESTELLA: Hello, Pip.

PIP: Estella! Why are you here?

ESTELLA: Bentley Drummle is dead. There was an accident with his horse. I'm here to say goodbye to Satis House.

PIP: And have you got a heart now?

ESTELLA: Yes, Pip, I have. But it is too late.

PIP: We're friends now, Estella.

ESTELLA: Yes, we're friends, Pip. But now we must say goodbye.

PIP: No, Estella. Now, I know the meaning of my life. Money isn't important. Being a gentleman isn't important. Great expectations aren't important. Friends are important. We are friends, Estella. We are together. (*He pauses*) This will not be our last goodbye.

THE END